THE PLAIN-ENGLISH GUIDE TO ECONOMIC SANCTIONS RISK ASSESSMENTS

Second Edition

By Heidi Hunter

Lil Abby Press

St. Paul, Minnesota

The Plain-English Guide to Economic Sanctions Risk Assessments
Second Edition

First Printing: August 2024

Second Printing: July 2025

Published by LilAbby Press
St. Paul, Minnesota
Printed in the United States of America

ISBN: 979-8-9994289-2-9 (paperback)
979-8-9994289-3-6 (ebook)

cover design by Heidi Hunter

Table of Contents

Disclaimer

The information provided in this book is for informational purposes only and is not intended to constitute legal advice. The author of this book is not an attorney, is not providing legal advice, and is not creating an attorney-client relationship with the reader.

Readers should not act or rely on any information in this book without seeking the advice of a lawyer. Any reliance upon the information contained in this guide is solely at the reader's own risk.

The author makes no representations or warranties about the completeness, accuracy, reliability, or suitability of the information in this book.

While every effort has been made to provide accurate and complete guidance, it's critical to understand that this guide does not guarantee an effective sanctions compliance program free from fines or penalties. Compliance with economic sanctions regulations is a complex and evolving area, and the effectiveness of any program depends on various factors, including the specific circumstances of the reader's business and the actions of relevant regulatory authorities. Therefore, the author cannot guarantee specific outcomes or results from implementing the suggestions provided in this guide. This information serves as a tool to develop and enhance your sanctions compliance program; however, the ultimate responsibility for compliance rests with the reader and their organization.

In no event shall the author be liable for any loss or damage whatsoever arising from, or in connection with, the use of the information contained in this book.

Introduction

Economic sanctions are powerful tools governments and international bodies use to influence the behavior of nations, organizations, and individuals. Navigating the complex sanctions landscape can be challenging for businesses of all sizes. Understanding and managing the risks associated with sanctions is crucial to ensure compliance and avoid severe penalties.

That's why I created *The Plain-English Guide to Economic Sanctions Risk Assessments, Second Edition,* now updated. This book aims to demystify the process of conducting a comprehensive assessment of your organization's economic sanctions risks, providing clear, actionable steps to safeguard your business. Whether you're a business owner, a compliance officer, or a compliance employee, this guide will equip you with the knowledge and tools needed to effectively manage sanctions risks.

If you're new to sanctions or want a refresher, the first book in this series, *The Plain-English Guide to Economic Sanctions,* provides a good overview. This guide assumes you are at least familiar with the concepts and terms presented in it.

Sanctions compliance isn't just about avoiding fines (though those can be substantial); it's also about ensuring the integrity of the financial system. It's also about protecting your business's reputation, maintaining customer trust, and operating ethically in a complex global environment. Violations can lead to multi-million-dollar civil and criminal penalties,[1] damage your brand, and invite scrutiny from regulators and business partners. By understanding these risks, you can take the necessary steps to safeguard your company and navigate the sanctions landscape with confidence.

This guide will mainly focus on conducting a risk assessment to comply with economic sanctions overseen by the Office of Foreign Assets Control (OFAC). You'll see terms like "economic sanctions," "OFAC sanctions," "trade sanctions," "sanctions regulations," "OFAC regulations," and "US sanctions" used interchangeably—they all refer to the same thing. OFAC has overseen many public enforcement actions and assessed numerous civil monetary penalties where deficiencies in a company's sanctions compliance program were identified as a cause of the violations.[2] OFAC considers risk assessment a key component of your economic sanctions compliance program.[3]

Throughout the book, we will use real-world examples and practical tips to illustrate each step in the process. You will learn how to assess your customers, products, services, and locations and how to develop and implement effective controls to manage the risks they pose. We will also discuss the importance of ongoing monitoring and regular reviews to ensure your risk assessment remains relevant and up-to-date with the changing sanctions landscape. We will walk through the completion of a sample risk assessment for a fictional company. By the end of this guide, you will have a solid understanding of creating and maintaining an effective economic sanctions risk assessment.

To assist you in completing your risk assessment, check out the companion workbook to this guide, *The Plain-English Guide to Economic Sanctions Risk Assessments Workbook.*

The recommendations in this guide draw on the author's experience, industry standards, and OFAC compliance guidance.

Definitions

Some of the terms referenced in this guide are defined below.

Beneficial Owner

The person who ultimately owns, benefits from, or controls an asset.

Blocking Program

An OFAC sanctions program that requires a sanctioned party's assets to be blocked or frozen. US persons are prohibited from doing business with them.

Business Partner/Third Party

Any external party you do business with. A business partner can be a vendor, a subcontractor, an attorney, a joint venture partner, a consultant, a distributor or wholesaler, a supplier, or an agent or representative acting on a company's behalf.

Comprehensive Sanctions

A trade embargo against a country. Most transactions are prohibited. Countries under comprehensive sanctions are Iran, Cuba, Syria[4], North Korea, and Russian-held areas of Ukraine, such as Crimea.

Control Gap

An internal control either does not exist or does not function properly.

Dual-Use Goods

Goods, software, and technology that can be used for both civilian and military purposes.

Economic Sanctions

The government's restrictions or penalties on individuals, entities, groups, governments, or countries to achieve particular foreign policy or national security goals.

Environmental Scanning

Also known as e-scanning. Environmental scanning is how you, as the sanctions compliance professional, stay updated on changes in economic sanctions regulations.

Freezing or Blocking Assets

Preventing a sanctioned party from accessing or using assets you hold that belong to them, such as a bank account or an insurance policy. Assets are deposited into a blocked bank account when possible.

Internal Controls

Internal controls are the processes, procedures, and measures that prevent and detect sanctions violations.

List-Based Sanctions

Programs where sanctioned parties are added to the Specially Designated Nationals (SDN) list. Most transactions with them are prohibited, and assets you hold that belong to them may need to be blocked.

Nexus

Transactions connected to the US, such as participation by a US party, sale of a US good or service, and transacting in US dollars or through the US financial system. Non-US persons carrying out transactions outside the US may be required to comply with US sanctions if those transactions have a US nexus.

The term is also used when referencing whether a particular transaction, claim, or policy has a connection to a sanctioned country, party, or good.

Office of Foreign Assets Control (OFAC)

The Office of Foreign Assets Control (OFAC), part of the US Department of the Treasury, oversees most US sanctions programs.

OFAC Regulations

OFAC incorporates sanctions laws and executive orders into its own regulations for a program, which are issued in the Code of Federal

Regulations (CFR). The CFR is where all rules implemented by the Federal government are published.

OFAC Sanctions

Sanctions administered by the Office of Foreign Assets Control (OFAC). You'll see terms like "economic sanctions," "OFAC sanctions," "trade sanctions," "sanctions regulations," "OFAC regulations," and "US sanctions" used interchangeably in this guide.

Risk Assessment

A risk assessment is a method for identifying, analyzing, and addressing a company's sanctions risks. It pinpoints any weaknesses in the program and lays out a plan to fix them.

Risk Category

Groups of similar types of risks, such as customers, products, services, geography, transactions, and third parties.

Risk Criteria

The measures used to evaluate the significance of a risk. They include inherent risk, residual risk, likelihood, and severity.

Risk Score

A categorical value (high, medium, and low) is assigned to a risk based on its assessed impact and likelihood. This score helps prioritize which risks need more immediate attention and action.

Root Cause

The main reason why a process failed.

Sanctioned Party/Specially Designated National (SDN)

An individual, company, organization, group, government, vessel, or aircraft sanctioned by OFAC and listed on the Specially Designated Nationals (SDN) list. Their assets are blocked, and US persons are generally prohibited from dealing with them.[5]

Sanctions Compliance Officer (SCO)

The person within an organization with ultimate responsibility for the sanctions compliance program.

Sanctions Compliance Program (SCP)

The policies, procedures, and controls that help a company comply with sanctions regulations.

Sanctions Compliance/Sanctions Compliance Team

The function within a company responsible for managing the policy, program, and controls related to sanctions compliance. The SCO is part of this function, and there may also be a separate team dedicated to sanctions (i.e., the sanctions compliance team).

Sanctions Program

All the laws, Executive Orders, OFAC regulations, guidance, licenses, and frequently asked questions governing restrictions against a specific country or activity. It governs what you can and cannot do.

Sanctions Risk

Potential threats or weaknesses that can result in violations of OFAC's regulations if not adequately managed by internal controls.

Scanning/Screening

Reviewing a customer or transaction to identify potential sanctions issues. This can involve scanning a customer or payee name against OFAC's watchlists or reviewing a transaction for a sanctions nexus.

The 50 Percent Rule

Entities majority-owned (50 percent or more) by one or more blocked persons, either through direct or indirect ownership, that are also considered sanctioned despite not being named on a watchlist.

US Person

US citizens anywhere in the world, US-incorporated businesses, including their foreign branches, people who are in the US for any reason, even if they are citizens of another country, and any persons transacting in the US financial system, US dollars, or US goods. All US persons must comply with OFAC regulations.

Watchlists

Watchlists are lists maintained by OFAC of sanctioned parties and the prohibitions against them. These watchlists can be SDN and non-SDN lists. These lists specify various prohibitions for sanctioned parties, from asset blocking and transaction bans (for those on the SDN lists) to targeted restrictions (for those on the non-SDN lists).

1
Brief Refresher on Economic Sanctions

Sanctions are restrictions or penalties that governments impose on countries, individuals, groups, governments, or industries to help achieve specific foreign policy and national security objectives. For example, the United States may prohibit US citizens from engaging in particular trade or financial activities, or other dealings, unless they obtain permission from OFAC or are expressly permitted to do so by law.[6] Since each sanctions program is based on different foreign policy and national security goals, prohibitions can vary from one program to another.[7]

At its simplest, economic sanctions mean you are not allowed to do business with certain countries or parties. Before proceeding with a business transaction, you must do your homework to identify any potential sanctions issues.

Many countries have their own sanctions laws. If your company conducts business in multiple countries, such as selling to foreign customers, trading internationally, or working with foreign business partners, you may need to comply with sanctions rules from several countries.

The Office of Foreign Assets Control (OFAC), a part of the US Department of the Treasury, oversees most US sanctions programs. Some trade sanctions are managed by different agencies, including the Department of State (DoS) and the Bureau of Industry and Security (BIS) within the Department of Commerce. These export control restrictions work in conjunction with OFAC's sanctions.

Most sanctions programs are established and administered through Executive Orders issued by the President, laws established by Congress, and regulations established by OFAC.

OFAC administers sanctions programs that encompass all laws, Executive Orders, OFAC regulations, guidance, licenses, and FAQs related to restrictions against a specific country or activity. Some programs target activities in certain countries, such as Cuba, while some target specific activities globally, such as narcotics trafficking and weapons proliferation.

A country-based program does not mean that only people in that country are sanctioned. Parties anywhere in the world can be sanctioned under any program, including persons in the US and those in your country. For example, the Russian Harmful Foreign Activities Program imposes sanctions against individuals and entities anywhere in the world involved in specified harmful foreign activities of the Russian Federation.[8]

Also, programs may not exist indefinitely. For example, Sudan used to have a trade embargo, but it was discontinued several years ago, and Sudan is currently subject to only minimal sanctions.

The best place to find all of these documents is on the specific program's page on the OFAC website, the link for which is provided under References.

OFAC's definition of a US person is broad and can extend to individuals and businesses outside the US in certain situations.

You are required to comply with US sanctions if one of the following conditions exist:

- You are covered under the definition of a US Person.
- You are conducting a transaction with a US nexus.
- You are conducting activity covered by OFAC's secondary sanctions.

You are a US Person and are covered by US sanctions in the following situations:

- US citizens anywhere in the world
- US-incorporated businesses, including their foreign branches
- people in the US for any reason, even if they are citizens of another country
- any party using the US financial system, US dollars, or US goods[9]

This means a foreign bank without US branches must also follow OFAC rules if it uses US dollars or the US financial system for a transaction.

There are situations where foreign parties may need to comply with US sanctions:

- US-nexus transactions
- secondary sanctions
- foreign subsidiaries of US entities for certain programs, namely Cuba, Iran, and North Korea

The term "sanctions" encompasses a wide range of actions that the United States can take against a country, government, person, group, or industry, depending on the specific activity the US seeks to stop. Generally, sanctions fall into three main categories: list-based sanctions, comprehensive country sanctions, and sectoral or trade sanctions.[10]

The most challenging part of complying with sanctions is when parties are considered sanctioned despite not appearing on any SDN or Non-SDN list. This can occur in a couple of ways.

First, some OFAC sanctions block categories of persons even if they do not appear on the SDN List.[11] For example, for the Venezuelan sanctions program, Executive Order 13884 blocks any person who meets the definition of the "Government of Venezuela."[12] Also, OFAC's Cuba sanctions prohibit most transactions with Cuban nationals.[13]

The second way is commonly referred to as the "50 Percent Rule."[14] This rule applies when a company is majority-owned (i.e., 50 percent or more) by one or more sanctioned parties. This includes both direct and indirect ownership. These entities are considered sanctioned even if they aren't on the SDN list.

No official government list of companies owned by sanctioned parties exists; however, some private companies, such as Dow Jones, create and maintain such lists.

Economic sanctions impact your entire organization—every employee, every department, and every business line—especially in global industries. The need to be knowledgeable about and comply with sanctions extends beyond compliance professionals. Employees handling tasks with a sanctions nexus must also understand and adhere to sanctions requirements.

This list isn't exhaustive, but it highlights key roles that may have a sanctions nexus that will need sanctions procedures and training within your organization:

- payment processors (such as a payment for goods or services, claim, refund, or vendor payment)
- originate a payment on an account
- open new accounts
- underwrite policies or loans
- conduct customer due diligence
- import or export goods
- conduct marine shipments

- contract with vendors or other business partners
- sell products or services
- hire staff
- claims adjustors
- product development
- legal/compliance
- customer service

Now that you have a solid refresher on how sanctions work, it's time to focus on preventing violations within your company. The next section kicks off with the most crucial step: building a robust economic sanctions compliance program.

These topics are explored in more detail in *The Plain-English Guide to Economic Sanctions,* the first book in the series.

2
Introduction to Risk Assessments

OFAC recommends that organizations take a risk-based approach to their sanctions compliance program (SCP). But what does that mean? To develop an effective SCP, you must evaluate and understand your company's specific sanctions challenges and vulnerabilities. This requires conducting a thorough assessment of your risk factors.

Before we discuss risk assessments in detail, it's important first to understand what risk is.

What Is Risk?

According to OFAC, sanctions risks are potential threats or vulnerabilities that, if ignored or not properly handled, can lead to violations of OFAC's regulations and negatively affect an organization's reputation and business.[15]

In other words, considering your company's unique situation, how likely is it that it may violate sanctions regulations when conducting business?

What Is a Risk Assessment

A sanctions risk assessment (SRA) is a method for identifying, analyzing, and addressing a company's sanctions risks. It pinpoints weaknesses in the compliance program and lays out a plan to fix them.

Why a Sanctions Risk Assessment Is Critical

The primary goal of an SRA is to evaluate and reduce the risk of sanctions violations, ensuring compliance with OFAC regulations. By identifying gaps and strengthening controls, an SRA ensures compliance with OFAC regulations, minimizes financial penalties for violations, and protects an entity's reputation in the marketplace.

Who Should Conduct One?

All entities should conduct an SRA, particularly those at higher risk for sanctions violations, such as:

- those that conduct business internationally, including professional services such as law, accounting, and consulting

- financial institutions such as banks, cryptocurrency firms, broker-dealers, mutual funds, and insurance companies
- businesses that sell, import, export, or ship goods
- entities that work as governmental contractors

However, all businesses, including small, single-owner entities, can benefit from even a basic assessment of their sanctions risk exposure.

Depending on its size, an entity can have multiple levels of SRAs. First and foremost, all organizations should have an enterprise-wide SRA encompassing all risks and controls for the entire company. However, individual departments or divisions within larger companies may have their own risk assessments ("sub-assessments") as part of an overall departmental risk assessment. The sanctions risks and controls identified in those sub-assessments should roll up into the enterprise-wide risk assessment.

Introduction to the Risk Assessment Case Study

As we progress through this guide, we will create a basic enterprise risk assessment for a fictional company. This company has implemented some sanctions controls, but no formal risk and controls assessment has been conducted.

Here is the link to download the final, completed risk assessment for our case study and a blank risk assessment template to use as you embark on your own SRA: https://easysanctions.wordpress.com/the-plain-english-guide-to-economic-sanctions-risk-assessments/.

3

Steps in the Risk Assessment Process

OFAC recommends that an entity develop a methodology to identify, analyze, and address its sanctions risks.[16] There is no one approach to conducting a risk assessment. However, the following steps, which will be explained in detail in the following chapters, provide a framework for identifying and analyzing all possible risks. This method will also allow an organization to take a holistic (i.e., entire entity) view of the company from top to bottom.

1. Scoping the business – Chapter 4
2. Identifying risk categories – Chapter 5
3. Identifying sanctions risks – Chapter 6
4. Establishing the risk criteria – Chapter 7
5. Calibrating the risk score – Chapter 8
6. Assessing risks – Chapter 9
7. Identifying controls – Chapter 10
8. Assessing controls – Chapter 11
9. Gap identification and remediation – Chapter 12
10. Documenting the risk assessment – Chapter 13
11. Follow-up / next steps – Chapter 13

The Plain-English Guide to Economic Sanctions Risk Assessments Workbook can also assist you in completing your first risk assessment with easy-to-use worksheets that cover every step in the process.

4
Scoping

The most important part of your risk assessment is the information-gathering phase, also known as "scoping." You can't conduct a risk assessment without first understanding all parts of your company. This means you must begin by identifying all of your organization's legal entities, business teams, functional units, departments, divisions, customers, products, services, supply chains, and geographies.

There are three ways to collect this information on your entity: (1) document gathering, (2) questionnaires, and (3) meetings or interviews.

Document Gathering

The best way to start your SRA project is to obtain as much information about your company as possible. This may include internal organizational charts, a listing of all legal entities, regulatory filings (such as with the SEC if you work for a public company), annual and semi-annual reports, procedural documents, information on the products you provide, your distribution channels, and where you do business.

These items may be readily available on your company's external website or an internal site (such as SharePoint). Otherwise, you may need to request them from co-workers. These documents will help you identify who to contact to get your questions answered and provide more specificity to your questions.

Questionnaires

A questionnaire should be developed to gather the information from each business unit you contact. While not all questions will be relevant for every department, a questionnaire will help ensure consistency of information collected and that no topics are overlooked with any group.

A sample questionnaire is included with the risk assessment template and gathers details on the risk criteria discussed in Chapter 5. You may need to define some terms in the questionnaire. For example, the term "dual-use goods," a well-known concept in sanctions, may not be familiar to most people.

You'll also want information about the type of data the business unit handles (like customer information, financial transactions, and sales data) and which system the data is stored on. This will assist you in verifying that you are scanning all pertinent data against OFAC watchlists.

In larger organizations, you may want to begin your SRA process by distributing the questionnaire for completion. After it is returned, you can contact the person who completed the questionnaire with any follow-up questions by email, phone, or meeting.

Meetings/Interviews

In smaller organizations, you may be able to meet (either face-to-face or virtually) with a representative from each unit of the company and address the questions in person. Meetings will also be most effective for questionnaire responses that require deeper dives.

Who Should Be Contacted

Every department within your company, including foreign locations, should be included in your risk assessment. If you don't know someone in the unit, start by contacting the manager and requesting that they appoint someone as your liaison for the SRA project. Don't forget to include corporate units such as accounts payable, information technology, and human resources in your risk assessment. Sanctions risk exists there, too.

Senior Management Buy-in

An SRA is a labor-intensive endeavor and involves multiple people across the company. Implementing changes resulting from the SRA will also necessitate employee buy-in of the new processes. That's why it's essential to have senior management support for your risk assessment project. With senior management's "sponsorship," employees contacted for your SRA project will understand they are expected to assist you.

At the outset of your SRA, have a senior manager (such as the chief compliance officer) email managers who report to them announcing the start of the sanctions risk assessment and that their teams' cooperation with the project is expected. This will smooth the way for contacting other employees for information. This will also demonstrate senior management's commitment to sanctions compliance, as recommended by OFAC.[17]

Case Study: Background on WeExport

You work for WeExport, a fictional organization. From your initial scoping, you learned the following information:

WeExport has 2,500 employees in the US, the UK, and China. WeExport builds and sells computer parts for high-end computer systems used by governmental agencies, schools, and entities in the military, defense, and aerospace industries. Its revenue was $25 million last year. The entity in the UK is a sales office for foreign customers and is legally organized as a branch of WeExport. The China site is a manufacturing facility organized as a WeExport subsidiary.

You've identified the following departments within the company: sales, finance, human resources, legal and compliance, information technology (IT), shipping and receiving, customer service, marketing, product development, procurement, manufacturing, and the individual sales channels—government and education, individuals, and industry. WeExport also has a team of three people who conduct sanctions compliance activities and report to the chief compliance officer.

5
Risk Categories

Your questionnaire will consist of questions regarding specific risk categories.

What Is a Risk Category

In a risk assessment, a "risk category" is a classification used to group similar types of risks. These categories help to organize and prioritize potential threats or vulnerabilities based on their nature and impact on the organization. Grouping risks into categories makes it easier to systematically evaluate and manage them.

What Categories Should Be Assessed

As recommended by OFAC, you should gather detailed information on your **customers, products, services, and locations**. However, there are several other risk categories you can also include, depending on your type of business:

- supply chains
- distribution channels
- counterparties/third-party associates
- types of transactions
- governmental contracts
- technology

For larger entities, you may want to assess these items at the corporate level and separately by business unit or location. For example, at my previous company, we evaluated the risk categories for our foreign entities and distinct business units of our domestic entities, such as group benefits insurance, personal insurance, commercial insurance, and treasury. I then rolled those up into an assessment at the corporate level.

At the most basic level, the goal is to identify which of your risk categories—or which items within those categories—pose the highest threat of a sanctions violation.

As discussed in the prior chapter, you gather information on these risk categories via your questionnaire, document review, and meetings.

When addressing these risk categories, you should also try to quantify them. For example, suppose you learn that customers primarily come from the government, education, and defense industries. In that case, you will want to know the approximate percentage from each sector. This is because each industry has a different amount of associated sanctions risk. If most customers are in the defense industry, then the overall customer risk to the company would be considered higher than if most customers were from the educational sector.

Below are several questions to ask during the scoping phase. These questions are also included in the risk assessment template included with this guide.

Customers

- Who are your customers?
- Are they individuals, small businesses, governments, or corporations?
- Do you have a steady base of customers, or do most customers conduct one-off transactions?
- What industries or sectors do your customers operate in?

Businesses pose a higher risk than individuals because it's easier to conceal the true ownership of a company. A stable customer base poses less risk, as you are familiar with their usual transaction patterns and can easily identify transactions that are out of the ordinary. On the other hand, new clients are riskier because you're unfamiliar with them and the types of transactions they'll carry out.

The industry in which a customer operates also affects their risk level. Customers in the military, defense, and technology sectors pose a higher sanctions risk than those in the food and clothing sectors. This is because OFAC imposes more sanctions on military and defense industries and technological goods than on humanitarian items, such as food and clothing.

Keep in mind that a customer can also be an internal department. Teams such as HR and IT will have internal, not external, customers. These customers should also be captured in your questionnaire.

Products

- Do you provide goods or services, or both?
- What specific products and services do you sell?
- Are the products considered "dual-use goods" (defined as used for both civilian and military purposes)?

Identify the various types of products you sell, as they carry different risk levels. For instance, if you sell financial products, allowing online account opening poses a higher risk than those requiring in-person verification. Similarly, certain goods may entail greater risk depending on their industry use. For example, office chairs typically pose a low risk. In contrast, laptops may pose a higher risk if your customers are military contractors rather than schools.

If you provide a service as your "product," consider whether the service is high-risk or is used by high-risk customers. For example, a business offering payday loans has a higher sanctions risk than a business offering plumbing services. For an internal department, such as finance, their "product" may be providing wire and ACH services or receiving payment for goods, transactions that can affect your company's sanctions risk.

Services

- What services do you offer your customers?
- How are your services delivered?

Services here differ from whether your product is a service.

Do you provide correspondent banking services, online account setup, Automated Clearing House (ACH), or wire transactions? All of these may pose a higher risk. Additionally, extending credit to your customers can also increase risk.

How the services are provided also affects risk. Online transactions or services provided through third-party service providers pose a higher risk than services provided in person by company employees. When you offer services online, it's harder to be sure who you're actually doing business with.

Geographic Jurisdiction

- Where do you have employees?
- Where do you do business (sell goods, have offices, or provide services)?
- Do you have any business partners (vendors, etc.) in foreign locations?
- What countries specifically?

Each country carries its own sanctions risk. Business conducted in higher-risk jurisdictions (explained more fully in Chapter 9) poses an elevated risk of sanctions violations to your company. You will want to identify the countries in which your products or services are sold, as well as a breakdown of their largest jurisdictions. For example, if you decide that China is a high-risk jurisdiction for your company, but only .01 percent of your sales are made there, will you want to focus all of your sanctions controls on that business, or will you want to focus them more on Russia, also considered a higher-risk jurisdiction, where 20 percent of your sales are?

Keep in mind that there can be variations in risk even within the United States. Areas of the US can be considered higher risk due to drug trafficking or money laundering concerns.

Supply Chains

- What suppliers do you use, and what components or materials do they supply?
- Do the suppliers source materials from foreign countries?
- Do the suppliers source materials from other entities?
- Where are your primary suppliers located (in what countries specifically)?
- Who engages or contracts with these suppliers?
- Who oversees these suppliers?

Suppliers can pose a high sanctions risk for an entity because they may obtain their source materials from sanctioned countries or providers, and you may not be aware of it. Foreign suppliers, in particular, may not be required to comply with OFAC and may not be familiar with all prohibitions. OFAC will fine companies that use those prohibited materials in their goods.[18] And yes, OFAC expects you to vet every company in the supply chain. So, if your supplier gets materials from a company that sources part of it from elsewhere, you must document all that information in the SRA questionnaire to assess that risk.

It is also possible that whoever engaged the supplier did not thoroughly review the supplier at the outset of the contract, including their sourcing of materials. A business unit engaging suppliers directly poses a greater concern than a separate procurement group whose job is to vet potential third-party partners for risk.

Someone within the company, whether in the business line or a procurement team, should oversee the contract and ensure compliance with its terms, including any clauses related to compliance with OFAC sanctions.

Distribution Channels / Wholesalers

- What channels do you distribute goods through?
- Do you use any distributors in foreign countries, and if so, what countries specifically?
- Do distribution channels go through any countries with trade embargoes (Iran, Syria, North Korea, Cuba, Russia, or Russian-held areas of Ukraine)?
- Who engages or contracts with these distributors, and what criteria are used to select them?
- Who oversees these distributors?

Distributors and wholesalers, similar to suppliers, can pose a high sanctions risk for an entity because they may sell your products in sanctioned countries, to sanctioned entities, or in countries where that specific good is prohibited for export. Additionally, the distributor or wholesaler serves as an intermediary between you and your customer. This may prevent an organization from knowing its customers well enough to identify if they are a sanctions concern, causing the company to rely on the distributor or wholesaler to conduct sufficient due diligence. Also, foreign distributors and wholesalers may not be required to comply with OFAC regulations and may not be familiar with all the prohibitions.

OFAC will penalize companies if their goods are sold in a prohibited manner. For example, your wholesaler in the Middle East could sell your products in Iran, where a US company is not permitted to export them, resulting in OFAC fines.[19]

Like a supplier, it is possible that whoever engaged the third party did not thoroughly review them at the outset of the contract, including where and to whom they sell or ship your goods. A business unit engaging third parties directly poses a greater concern than a separate procurement team whose job is to vet potential third-party partners for risk.

Someone within the company, whether in the business line or a procurement team, should oversee the contract and ensure compliance with its terms, including any clauses related to compliance with OFAC sanctions and where your company's goods can and can't be sold.

Counterparties/Third-Party Associates

- Do you use any third-party business partners, including counterparties and vendors?
- What services do these third parties provide?
- Are any located in foreign countries, or do they provide services in foreign countries (what countries specifically)?
- Who engages or contracts with these third parties, and what criteria are used to select them?
- Who oversees these third parties?
- Do any of these third parties use subcontractors?

Counterparties, vendors, and third-party business partners (such as law firms or consultants) pose similar risks to suppliers and distribution partners. Suppose a vendor subcontracts some of the services they provide to you, and the subcontractor operates in a foreign country. This can pose a higher sanctions risk to your company than if the contractor provided the services themselves. At my previous firm, one vendor subcontracted work to independent contractors in Belarus. After the start of the Russian conflict, when Belarus became subject to sanctions, we had to decide if we wanted that exposure.

Additionally, a third party operating on your company's behalf in a foreign country (like a consulting firm hired to generate business) increases your company's risk. They might do business with sanctioned parties or governments, or bribe other entities to bring you business.

Types of Transactions

- What transactions are conducted by the department?
- What is the volume of the transactions?
- What is the value of the transactions (high, medium, low)?
- What is the frequency of customer transactions (regular/routine, sporadic, or one-off)?
- Can transactions be conducted on behalf of third parties or anonymous parties?
- Can the transaction have a counterparty, beneficiary, or intermediary (in other words, does the transaction involve or is for the benefit of someone other than your customer)?
- Are any transactions conducted in cash or cryptocurrency?
- Are any transactions (such as electronic funds transfers) to or from foreign countries?

Transactions involve the transfer of goods, services, or funds. They can pose an elevated sanctions risk to an organization if they involve a foreign country, a foreign bank, or a third party, such as an intermediary or counterparty you have not vetted.

Sanctioned parties will often use an intermediary to conduct transactions on their behalf. If a customer buys goods to be shipped to a country where they don't operate or buys goods that don't match their business (like a fashion retailer purchasing circuit boards), it could be a red flag that they're acting for an unknown third party.

High-value transactions can involve more risk, as they typically involve higher-value goods that sanctioned parties or money launderers may desire.

Cash and cryptocurrency transactions are high risk because you don't know where the funds came from or where they are going to. Cash and cryptocurrency are popular methods that sanctioned parties and criminals use to conduct transactions.

Finally, consider the volume of these transactions. Do your customers engage in many transactions or just a few? That can also affect risk.

Government Contracts

- Does the firm contract with federal, state, or foreign governments to provide goods or services?
- What foreign governments do you have contracts with?

Government contracts may be considered low-risk, but they can still pose a risk to your company. For example, your contract with the government may state that you can't do business with certain parties that may or may not be sanctioned. My last company was a government contractor. In some cases, we had to certify that we weren't doing business with certain entities with ties to China or the Iranian energy sector, some of which were not sanctioned by OFAC.

In some countries, the entire country (such as Iran), a governmental regime (such as the government of Venezuela), or specific governmental departments (such as the Myanmar Directorate of Procurement in Myanmar/Burma) may be sanctioned, which can present difficulty in identifying allowable governmental business.

In addition, an organization must exercise greater caution in negotiating these contracts to ensure that nothing is offered or received that could be considered a bribe under US or local regulations. Foreign governmental entities can include state-owned enterprises, such as hospitals or universities, that may be your target customers.

Technology

- What data does your department maintain (customer data, transactions, vendor information, account data, sales data, etc.)?
- What application or system is this data maintained on?

These questions will help you identify the data you need to scan and verify that it is being checked against sanctions watchlists.

Case Study: Risk Categories for WeExport

Conducting the SRA for WeExport, you've obtained the following information:

Customers: IT companies that build high-end computers for governments, education, and defense/military/aerospace industries.

Approximately 45 percent of the business is defense, military, or aerospace; 25 percent is other government; 15 percent is education; and 15 percent is in miscellaneous industries. Customers are relatively stable, as a limited number of well-known companies are building these systems. WeExport does not conduct a beneficial ownership review of its customers.

Products: Parts used in high-end computers. They can be considered dual-use goods.

Services: WeExport provides warranty and repair services through third-party vendors.

Geographic Jurisdiction: Products are sold to US-based (approximately 50 percent) and foreign customers. Of the foreign customers, China is the largest purchaser (25 percent). Other countries include Canada, India, Germany, and South Africa.

Suppliers: WeExport has three suppliers for materials used in its computer parts, two of which are located in China and India. The one in China has a third-party supplier that it can use to source materials.

Distributors/Wholesalers: WeExport uses three distributors/wholesalers in the US, Germany, and the Middle East.

Third Parties: WeExport outsources payroll and IT services. IT services are conducted from India.

Transactions: Frequent, regular, medium-sized bulk purchases of computer parts. Medium-dollar-value transactions, as the parts are not high-value items. Transactions are not always with the final beneficial owner of the goods (as wholesalers are involved).

Government Contracts: WeExport has contracts with the US government and the French government.

Technology: An automated scanning system has been implemented. Employee data in the HR system and vendor onboarding data in their procurement system are not being scanned against sanctions watchlists. Payments to vendors and other third parties, such as wholesalers and distributors, are being scanned from their accounts payable system. Customer names are checked when an order is placed.

6
Sanctions Risks

Now that you have identified and gathered information on your company's risk categories, you need to identify the specific sanctions-related risks your company may face.

Sanctions Risk

As mentioned earlier, sanctions risk refers to potential threats or weaknesses that can lead to violations of OFAC regulations if not properly managed by internal controls.

Sanctions risks differ from risk categories. Risk categories influence the sanctions risk score, either raising or lowering it.

Identifying Sanctions Risks

Brainstorm all the ways your organization could violate sanctions without any controls in place. This will be your universe of risks that you must mitigate.

Some sanctions risks that your company may face include (this is not an exhaustive list):

- The company's sanctions compliance program is insufficient to comply with economic sanctions.
- The company does not identify sanctions issues.
- Sanctioned customers are not identified.
- Transactions that violate sanctions are conducted.
- Technology is insufficient to enable sanctions compliance.
- Employees don't understand sanctions.
- Required OFAC reports are not filed.
- The company does not block assets of an SDN or reject a transaction for an SDN when required by the regulation.
- New sanctions requirements are not identified and implemented.
- Third parties may put the company at risk for sanctions violations.
- Documents are not retained for the required amount of time.

Broken Controls

When framing sanctions risks in your SRA, ensure they are not phrased as broken controls (i.e., a missing or defective control). For example, "we don't scan our customers" is not a risk but a broken control. The risk is "sanctioned customers are not identified" or "we do business with sanctioned parties." Scanning would be a way to control those risks, and not performing it is a gap. Another example is "employees aren't trained in sanctions." That is, again, a broken control, the control being "training." The actual risk is that employees don't understand sanctions, so they don't follow procedures.

In the next chapter, we'll begin discussing how to assign values to the risk categories and the sanctions risks.

Case Study: Sanctions Risks for WeExport

WeExport identified the sanctions risks listed above as the sanctions risks for their company.

7
Risk Criteria

Now that we have identified our risk categories and sanctions risks, we must establish how to measure them. This is done using risk criteria. This chapter will discuss the criteria used to assess the risk categories, sanctions risks, and controls.

What Is Risk Criteria

Risk criteria are the measures used to evaluate the significance of a risk. In a risk assessment, this includes inherent risk, residual risk, likelihood, and severity.

Inherent Risk

Inherent risk is the risk level before implementing any controls. In simpler terms, it's how likely a sanctions violation will occur without controls. It takes into consideration both the likelihood and severity of a risk. For example, a company with high-risk customers, products, services, and geography might have a high inherent risk level for the sanctions risk: "sanctioned customers are not identified." A local retail business would likely have a low inherent risk for the same risk, since it would have less exposure to higher-risk customers and locations.

Residual Risk

Residual risk is the likelihood that a sanctions violation will occur after the controls are performed (controls are discussed in Chapter 10). Your goal is that the controls will reduce the inherent risk. A company with a high inherent risk for "sanctioned customers are not identified" may find that their residual risk falls to medium or even low with robust, effective controls that detect potential sanctioned parties. A company with few or ineffective controls may find that the residual risk remains high.

If the residual risk exceeds your risk tolerance with the current controls, then procedures must be redesigned to be more effective, or other processes must be developed. However, your goal is not to completely eliminate all risk, as that would not be possible.

Risk tolerance refers to the level of risk you are willing to accept in your sanctions program, considering the potential for violations. For example, a residual risk of high may not fall within your tolerance (and it shouldn't), but a medium residual risk may be acceptable.

Although not all assessments include them, the following two criteria can also be used in your risk assessment. They will help you evaluate your company's risks more accurately.

Likelihood

Likelihood is the probability of a risk occurring. It is related to inherent risk, but not the same. For the local retailer example above, you may have a high inherent risk for the sanctions risk: "sanctioned customers are not identified," as you don't have any sanctions controls in place. However, being a store that operates primarily locally, the likelihood of encountering a customer or transaction with a sanctions nexus is low. Assessing both criteria will help you design the appropriate level of control for your risks.

You may not want to focus on risks with a low likelihood of occurrence and focus your initial efforts on those with a high likelihood. You will use the assessment of your risk categories to determine the likelihood of a sanctions risk violation. For example, if you have assessed the customer risk as high, the likelihood of a violation for the risk "sanctioned customers are not identified" is likely or highly likely.

Severity

Severity is the potential impact or consequences of a sanctions-related violation. This includes financial losses, legal penalties, reputational damage, and operational disruptions. Assessing severity helps organizations understand the seriousness of each risk and prioritize their mitigation efforts accordingly.

For example, you may decide that the severity of the sanctions risk, "the company's sanctions compliance program is insufficient to comply with economic sanctions," is critical because a violation would likely lead to significant legal penalties, reputational damage from an OFAC fine, possible legal fees for lawsuits, and operational disruptions as you work quickly to fix the program.

To quantify severity, look at prior published OFAC notices and see what the fines were, what the aggravating factors were (aggravating factors increase the penalty, which is a concern if you have the same control gap), and what types of violations were publicized (not all OFAC violations lead to a public notice). You can search online to see what publicity is generated when a company is fined to assess possible reputational impact. Also, consider whether you have to report violations in public filings, such as annual reports or SEC filings. You can even use prior litigation or penalties your company received in the past as a benchmark.

Some companies prepare a formal matrix (sometimes called a "heat map") and mark where each of the sanctions risk categories falls. I have included a template for one in the risk assessment template, although there are several examples on the internet.[20]

8
Risk Scores

We have one last step before we begin assessing the risks—defining how we will measure our risk categories (Chapter 5), sanctions risks (Chapter 6), and risk criteria (Chapter 7). This is done using a risk score.

What Is a Risk Score

A risk score is a categorical value assigned to a risk based on its assessed impact and likelihood of occurrence. This score helps prioritize which risks need more immediate attention and action.

When the risk categories, sanctions risks, and risk criteria are assessed, they are scored as **high, medium, or low**, which will be used to determine the company's overall risk level. I also recommend using medium-high and medium-low for larger companies with diverse risks that need more precise measurement.

Below are general definitions of high, medium, and low risk:

High risk: Indicates the significant possibility of a sanctions violation occurring in the current state. Includes a substantial potential for severe consequences. These risks require urgent attention and robust controls to mitigate them.

Medium risk: Denotes a moderate possibility of a sanctions violation occurring in the current state with a modest potential for financial or reputational impact. These risks require regular monitoring and effective controls, but are less urgent than high-risk ones.

Low risk: Suggests a low likelihood of occurrence in the current state, with minimal potential for financial or reputational impact. These risks require routine checks but generally do not need immediate or intensive controls.[21]

To assess likelihood and severity, you can use the high/medium/low scale to stay consistent with how inherent and residual risks are evaluated and to avoid confusion. However, we will use the more commonly used scores in this guide.

Likelihood is scored from highly likely to possible to highly unlikely, and severity ranges from negligible to medium to critical. These scores generally correspond to the high, medium, and low definitions above.

9
Assessing Risks

Using the risk categories from Chapter 5, the sanctions risks from Chapter 6, the risk criteria from Chapter 7, and the risk scores from Chapter 8, you are now ready to assess your organization's sanctions-related risks. You will assess the risk categories first, then use those assessments to analyze the sanctions risks.

How Risk Score Is Determined

The sanctions risk for each criterion must be assessed and given a score of high, medium, or low to arrive at the company's final risk level. So, the question on your mind is likely: How do I determine whether something is high, medium, or low risk? This determination will vary from entity to entity and is somewhat subjective, based on the assessor's knowledge of sanctions and their familiarity with the company and its industry. It can depend on factors such as the financial impact, whether there would be publicity, whether your company operates globally, and whether the industries it operates in are frequently targeted for sanctions.

For example, you may decide that a risk is low if it involves a loss of under five thousand dollars, does not require reporting, and is unlikely to be publicized. On the other hand, you may decide a risk is high if it would involve a penalty of over $1 million, lead to potential lawsuits, and be publicized globally.

Making this assessment more complicated, a spectrum of risks may be identifiable within the same category. For example, some customers (individuals) may be at lower risk than others (military customers). This is why it's essential to try to quantify these risk categories. If 95 percent of your customers are individuals, your customer risk will be lower than if 95 percent of your customers are military customers.

For those without experience with risk assessments, the Federal Financial Institutions Examination Council (FFIEC)[22] BSA/AML Manual provides a suitable, easy-to-read matrix with examples of what to consider high, medium, or low risk. OFAC also uses this matrix.[23]

Assess the risk categories first, then use those assessments to analyze the sanctions risks. You should also consider assessing risk by individual departments or business units to identify those parts of the organization with higher sanctions risk.

Risk Category Analysis

Let's apply these criteria to a sample of our WeExport risk categories in Table 1. Your assessment of these risk categories may differ, and that's perfectly acceptable. Remember, a significant part of this process is subjective. The key takeaway from this exercise is to stimulate your thinking about all the various factors and how they interact to determine a company's risk rating.

Table 1. Risk Category Analysis for WeExport

Risk Category	Risk Score & Rationale
Customers	medium-high
	Most of WeExport's customers are businesses that build high-end computers for governments, education, and defense/military/aerospace industries. Nearly half of the business is in a high-risk industry. Some products are sold through wholesalers, making the ultimate end user unknown to WeExport. This initially suggests high customer risk. However, the other customer categories are not considered high-risk for sanctions. Also, WeExport has determined that customers are relatively stable, with a limited, well-known number of companies building these types of systems. These factors lower the risk. However, since WeExport does not conduct beneficial ownership reviews of its customers or identify those sold to by wholesalers, customer risk is considered medium-high.
Product	high
	The product, computer parts, falls in a category frequently restricted by OFAC across various sanctions programs. These goods are often used in sanctioned industries like the military and defense, making them dual-use goods. Therefore, the product risk is considered high.

Table 1 (continued).

Risk Category	Risk Score & Rationale
Geography	medium-high
	WeExport operates globally, with manufacturing in China, a higher-risk country. They also have distributors, wholesalers, and suppliers in foreign countries, including higher-risk areas like China, India, and the Middle East. Half of their products are sold to US-based entities, reducing geographic risk. Among the other countries that procure their goods, China is the highest-risk location, with about 25 percent of sales. This means 75 percent of their products are sold in lower-risk regions, reducing the overall risk. However, their domestic and foreign wholesalers can sell to customers and countries unknown to WeExport, so the geographic risk remains medium-high.
Third Parties	medium-high
	Two of WeExport's suppliers are in China and India, considered higher-risk jurisdictions. Additionally, WeExport has one distributor/wholesaler in a high-risk area (the Middle East). The company also outsources payroll and IT services, with one subcontracted to a facility in India. WeExport considers the number of third parties it uses to be average for its industry. However, using third parties for distribution and supplies, including one in a high-risk area, increases the risk because there is less visibility into the other parties involved in the transaction. While China and India are higher-risk jurisdictions, they are not the highest-risk areas globally. This, along with the moderate number of outsourcing relationships, puts the risk in the medium-high range.
Transactions	medium-high
	WeExport has frequent, regular, medium-sized bulk purchases of goods. Most transactions are with parties whom WeExport deals with regularly, so they are transacting with mostly known parties. The dollar value per transaction is medium-sized. All this points to a medium risk. However, WeExport doesn't accept cash but will accept cryptocurrency in certain instances, which is the highest-risk payment method because criminals often use it due to its anonymity. This raises the risk to medium-high.

Reviewing the risk scores for these categories, it appears so far that WeExport probably has an overall sanctions risk in the medium-high range. Let's next look at the sanctions risks.

Sanctions Risks Analysis

Now, we will assess the inherent risk, likelihood, and severity of each sanctions risk for the WeExport case study. I have selected a few of the sanctions risks identified in Chapter 6 for analysis in Table 2. The remainder are included in the completed SRA.

Table 2. Sanctions risk analysis for WeExport

<table>
<tr><th>Sanctions Risk</th><th>Inherent Risk</th><th>Likelihood</th><th>Severity</th></tr>
<tr><td rowspan="2">Employees don't understand sanctions or follow sanctions procedures.</td><td>High</td><td>Highly likely</td><td>Critical</td></tr>
<tr><td colspan="3">Sanctions are complex regulations, and most employees don't work with them or receive training on them. Therefore, the likelihood of employees not understanding sanctions is high. WeExport's risk categories were assessed to be in the medium-high range, making employee knowledge of sanctions vital to compliance. This will lead to a high likelihood of a sanctions violation, incurring high fines and penalties.</td></tr>
<tr><td rowspan="2">Third parties may put the company at risk for sanctions violations.</td><td>Medium-high</td><td>Likely</td><td>Medium</td></tr>
<tr><td colspan="3">WeExport works with several third parties for supplies, sales, and outsourced processes, some of which are in foreign countries not subject to OFAC regulations. The number of third parties is relatively low, and most are not located in high-risk areas. Therefore, the probability of a violation occurring is likely rather than highly likely, given the moderate number of suppliers, distributors, and third-party vendors. An OFAC violation by a third party would expose WeExport to fines and penalties, reputational risk, and potential for lawsuits. Since most transactions are moderate in size and value, the severity of a penalty would likely be less monetarily than higher-value transactions.</td></tr>
</table>

Table 2 (continued).

Sanctions Risk	Inherent Risk	Likelihood	Severity
Required documents are not retained for the required amount of time.	Medium-low	Unlikely	Low
	Companies, including WeExport, function in a digital environment and naturally have computer systems in place that save documents. Therefore, the probability of a pertinent sanctions-related document not being available when necessary is low. If sanctions-related documentation is unavailable during an OFAC inquiry or when assessing a possible violation, that would increase the risk of fines and penalties, increasing the severity. However, basic computerization would manage this risk, so the severity is considered low.		
Sanctioned customers are not identified.	Medium-high	Highly likely	Critical
	WeExport has a mostly stable base of regular customers with whom they are familiar, so the risk isn't high. However, WeExport's customers are in high-risk industries and can be located in foreign countries. Also, they sell through third parties and rely on those entities to vet purchasers of WeExport's goods, which increases risk. The probability of a sanctioned customer being identified without controls is low. Having a sanctioned customer could lead to fines and penalties from OFAC, reputational damage, loss of business, and lawsuits from your customer if you cancel a contract. Since there are multiple ways that having a sanctioned customer can cause a loss to WeExport, the severity is assessed at the highest level, which is critical.		

Assessing Department or Business Unit Risk

Your risk assessment should also evaluate the sanctions risk of individual departments or business units within your company. This helps identify which units need the most robust controls. For example, a high-risk business unit solely relying on automated screening may require additional controls (such as a referral process) to reduce risk. Or, a foreign unit might need to comply with multiple sanctions regimes.

For each department, evaluate the inherent risk, likelihood, and severity of potential sanctions violations. Later, you'll identify the controls the unit relies on, assess those controls, and determine the residual sanctions risk for that business unit. Ideally, this should be part of the unit's individual risk assessment, and you can include these results in the company-wide SRA. However, always review the unit's results and judgments. If a unit believes its sanctions risk is low, but you disagree, that gap needs to be discussed.

Let's look at an example by analyzing three of WeExport's departments in Table 3. The remainder are included in the completed SRA.

Table 3. Business unit risks of WeExport

Business Unit	Inherent Risk	Likelihood	Severity
Sales - Education	medium-low	unlikely	medium
	Education is a low-risk business unit, as sanctions rarely affect this industry. Therefore, the likelihood of a violation is unlikely and of medium severity should one occur.		
Shipping and Receiving	high	highly likely	critical
	Shipping and receiving are considered high risk because they ship globally, there are many parties to a shipment, goods can be shipped to countries where they are prohibited, and some shipping routes can go through sanctioned jurisdictions. Therefore, the likelihood is high that a sanctions violation would occur without controls, and the severity of the penalty would have a critical impact on the company.		
Procurement	medium-high	likely	high
	Procurement is considered a higher-risk area because it is responsible for identifying, contracting with, and monitoring third parties with whom WeExport does business. The number of third parties is not high, and most are not in high-risk areas, lowering inherent risk slightly. However, several of these third parties are located in foreign countries. Therefore, the likelihood of a violation absent any controls is likely to have a high severity of impact.		

What Countries Are Higher Risk

You may wonder how to identify which countries pose higher risks. There are several methods to consider, and a country that ends up being rated high risk according to one or more of these methods should be regarded as high risk:

- Countries with OFAC sanctions programs[24] should be considered higher risk. Those countries with trade embargoes—Iran, Syria, Cuba, North Korea, and Russian-held regions of Ukraine, such as Crimea—are the highest risk, as most business activity in these countries is prohibited. Also, consider countries that are allied with these highest-risk countries. For example, China and India are two countries that are friendly toward Russia. Even though India doesn't have a sanctions program, it may be considered at increased risk compared to a country like the UK.
- The Financial Action Task Force (FATF)[25] lists countries on "black" and "gray" lists for anti-money laundering deficiencies. These countries can be considered high-risk due to their lack of controls over fraud and abuse. Currently, Iran, Myanmar, and North Korea are on the black list.
- Transparency International[26] is a great resource that calculates a corruption index and ranks countries based on their level of corruption. Download their Corruption Perceptions Index spreadsheet to identify if a country you are doing business in is considered corrupt. According to their 2024 index, Denmark is the least corrupt country, while South Sudan is the most corrupt.
- Current events should also factor into your geographic risk analysis. While there are no sanctions programs over Israel, the fact that it is a political hot spot should move it toward the top of your risk list if you do business there.
- As mentioned, some areas of the US are considered higher risk than others. This may help organizations that only operate domestically to assess their geographical risk. These jurisdictions can be identified using the maps of the High Intensity Drug Trafficking Area (HIDTA)[27]

and High Intensity Financial Crimes Area (HIFCA).[28] Customers located in these areas are generally considered at increased risk.

You will notice we didn't assess residual risk in this chapter. Residual risk will be evaluated once the controls are identified and assessed. The next chapter discusses identifying and assessing the controls to help mitigate all the sanctions risks you've identified.

10
Identify Controls

Ensuring that you have the appropriate processes and procedures to adequately address the risks identified in your analysis is crucial for the success of your program. Without suitable and effective safeguards, your program will not succeed, and your company could face fines and penalties. If you are just starting to develop a sanctions program, you may not have any controls in place yet. Or, controls might be scattered throughout the company.

What Are Controls

Internal controls are the processes, procedures, and measures that prevent and detect sanctions violations. Internal controls will reduce your sanctions risks. You may have a good idea of what controls exist within the company from the scoping phase of the SRA.

If you have a risk where you can't identify a mitigating control, you have a **control gap** that must be resolved. This will be discussed in Chapter 11.

What Controls Should Be Implemented

Your controls will vary depending on your industry, size, and global scope. However, these are some of the critical controls you will want to implement:

- a written sanctions program
- an economic sanctions policy
- program oversight
- automated scanning/screening of customers and transactions
- customer due diligence
- third-party due diligence
- training
- contract wording
- risk assessment
- auditing and testing
- written procedures
- environmental scanning

For more details on implementing these controls, refer to *The Plain-English Guide to Developing an Economic Sanctions Program* (the second book in this series). Not having one of these controls in your sanctions compliance program may be considered a control gap.

Below are basic expectations for these controls to assist you in assessing the effectiveness and sufficiency of your controls.

Sanctions Program

A sanctions compliance program (SCP) comprises the policies, procedures, and controls that help a company comply with sanctions regulations. It should be in writing and periodically reviewed and updated. Depending on your company's size and whether it operates worldwide or just in the United States, your program might include some or all of these elements:

- economic sanctions policy
- written procedures
- risk assessment
- responsibility and oversight for the program
- internal controls
- sanctions clauses in contracts
- environmental scanning to identify new and updated sanctions requirements
- training
- auditing and testing of the program to ensure it's operating effectively

Policy

The cornerstone of a sanctions compliance program is an economic sanctions policy. The policy outlines your company's commitment to sanctions compliance and briefly describes the procedures and controls for compliance.

Sections to include in your policy:

- senior management's commitment to fostering a culture of compliance
- pertinent definitions for key terms such as sanctions, sanctioned parties, prohibited transactions, etc.
- sanctions laws applicable to your company, both domestic and foreign

- potential penalties to the company and the individual for non-compliance
- who the policy applies to in the company, and whether third parties such as vendors and business partners must comply with your policy
- the person responsible for the program and their duties
- that a risk assessment is conducted
- high-level description of internal controls
- who will receive sanctions training
- testing and auditing of the program
- methods to report potential violations

Program Oversight

Someone within the company should be responsible for overseeing sanctions compliance. This includes oversight for all aspects of the program, direct supervision of the sanctions compliance team if there is one, and indirect oversight of any additional staff performing sanctions-related duties. In larger companies, the person may be called the sanctions compliance officer (SCO).

Scanning/Screening

Scanning involves checking a party's name (customer, vendor, employee, payee, etc.) against sanctions watchlists to see if there is a match or reviewing transactions for a sanctions nexus.

An automated scanning application is ideal for a sanctions program. If properly set up, it should require minimal intervention. Companies that offer these applications include Lexis Nexis, Moody's, and Computer Services, Inc. (CSI).

Everyone you do business with should be scanned. While scanning customers and payees may seem obvious, you should also include your employees, vendors, account beneficiaries, parties from whom you receive payments, joint venture partners, and other third parties and business partners. If you ship goods, you should also scan details such as the vessel name, freight forwarder, and shipping company, among other data points.

If you sell high-risk or dual-use goods, you should screen them against their destination to ensure they are not prohibited from being exported there.

Scan all transactions before completion, including payments made or received. Scan customers before opening accounts, issuing policies, or shipping goods. Scan third-party business partners or vendors before finalizing the contract.

Periodically rescan customers and vendors, even if there have been no recent transactions. OFAC prohibits maintaining accounts and contracts with sanctioned parties.

Use OFAC's sanctions lists, including SDN and non-SDN lists. For foreign operations, include foreign government sanctions watchlists for relevant countries. A comprehensive global sanctions watchlist is necessary for companies operating in multiple countries. Dow Jones offers a list that can be integrated into your screening solution.

Customer Due Diligence

Customer due diligence means getting to know your customers to understand their risks. This includes checking their names against sanctions watchlists, identifying who owns and runs the customer's business (beneficial ownership) and scanning them, and looking for any sanctions-related red flags in their business activities, such as negative news, fines, or connections to sanctioned parties.

Legal Entities and Ultimate Beneficial Ownership (UBO)

Various legal entities, such as LLCs, LPs, LLPs, and PLCs, are commonly used by sanctioned parties to conceal their assets. These entities often obscure ownership details, especially when incorporated in jurisdictions such as Jersey or the Cayman Islands, which have opaque registration rules. Sanctioned individuals may further complicate matters by structuring these entities to be owned by other entities, making uncovering true ownership challenging. Some companies, such as Dow Jones and LexisNexis, have compiled databases of the ultimate beneficial owners of various legal entities. Additionally, entities are now required to file beneficial ownership information with the Financial Crimes Enforcement Network (FinCEN) under the Beneficial Ownership Information Reporting Rule.[29]

However, these databases aren't infallible. When dealing with customers operating under one of these legal entities, requesting information and documentation of ultimate beneficial ownership during customer due diligence is essential to ensure compliance and avoid engaging with sanctioned parties.

Third-Party Due Diligence

Similar due diligence steps should be performed on your vendors and other third parties, such as wholesalers, suppliers, and distributors. This includes identifying beneficial ownership, scanning key parties (e.g., executives or board members), and reviewing the countries in which they will be working under your company's contract.

However, vendor management doesn't end after the contracting phase. If the contract with the vendor lasts for several years, you should perform ongoing monitoring. The frequency will depend on the vendor's risk. Less frequent monitoring can be done on smaller contracts with US companies. More frequent reviews (such as annually) should be conducted for large contracts with companies performing key activities (such as payment processing) overseas.

During your periodic monitoring, verify that the information gathered at onboarding is up-to-date, rescan all the names against the watchlists, conduct a negative news review for the time since onboarding, and verify that the countries where the work is being performed have not become sanctioned.

Training

Everyone in a company should have basic knowledge and training on sanctions. If you decide not to train everyone, at least train staff whose jobs are directly affected by sanctions, such as those who onboard new customers or process payments. It's also a good idea to offer training to third parties, such as vendors, distributors, and suppliers, so they understand your expectations for sanctions compliance.

Training can be provided in various formats, including in-person sessions, virtual meetings, PowerPoint presentations, programs from learning platforms like True Office/Learning Pool, periodic emails, and articles posted on internal websites like SharePoint.

Keep sanctions training brief and straightforward. Generally, twenty to thirty minutes is enough, but no more than an hour is recommended for those who require in-depth training.

Track the training details: what was provided, when, and to whom.

People in key roles related to sanctions need at least annual training and possibly a refresher or more intensive training during the year. For those who only need to know the basics, a refresher every two to three years should suffice.

Contract Wording

You should include sanctions exclusion clauses in contracts and insurance policies. Typically, your sanctions exclusion clause would state that the contract or policy is void and that payment will not be made if it breaches sanctions in any of these jurisdictions: your own, the other party's, and the jurisdiction(s) where the transactions are conducted.

Similarly, if goods are sold to a third party, like a wholesaler, the contract should specify that the goods cannot be resold in a way that breaches sanctions, such as selling to a sanctioned party or country.

Risk Assessment

The risk assessment you are conducting now can be considered a program control.

Auditing and Testing

Auditing and testing are critical to ensuring that procedures are performed correctly to maintain compliance with sanctions. Testing may include checking closed sanctions alerts to see if they were properly resolved, reviewing third-party compliance with contracts, and testing controls performed by other departments (like accounts payable manually scanning payees) to ensure they are working adequately. Additionally, internal audits of the program are necessary.

Written Procedures

The process for performing the sanctions controls should be clearly documented in writing. This shows OFAC, auditors, and internal parties, such as the CCO, that procedures are in place and how they work, and it serves as a valuable training tool for new staff.

Procedures should be step-by-step, as this document will help train new staff and serve as a reminder for current staff on the correct process. Use screenshots if the document explains how to use a system. For example, in a procedure detailing how to clear alerts in your sanctions screening system, include screenshots from your application.

These procedures should be stored in a shared online site where employees can easily access them.

Here's a list of procedures that should be in writing:

- how to review and clear alerts from a scanning application
- how and when to manually scan business
- when other departments need to refer business to the sanctions compliance team or the SCO for review
- what steps to take if a customer is sanctioned
- how to conduct a risk assessment
- how to escalate sanctions issues (such as a potential violation)
- how and when to contact OFAC (filing blocked asset and rejected transaction reports, applying for specific licenses, filing a voluntary self-disclosure, etc.)

Environmental Scanning

Sanctions can change regularly, so you must monitor them daily for updates to the watchlists, changes to sanctions programs, or the implementation of new programs.

You should develop a written procedure documenting how you will conduct the scanning, record your findings, and develop and implement new processes in response to new regulations.

Third Parties and Controls

A control that an external party performs for you is not a control for your program. You can't depend solely on an external third party, like a bank, to carry out a control for you. Instead, you must either (1) perform the control yourself (such as screening a payee before sending a payment to the bank) or (2) oversee the third party's completion of the control procedure.

For example, as part of your compliance testing program, you may periodically audit payments made by a third-party vendor to ensure they are being properly screened. While you can acknowledge in the risk assessment that a third party performs a control, your company's control is overseeing the third party's actions. OFAC doesn't permit a company to rely solely on a third party to fulfill its sanctions requirements without oversight.[30]

Technology Is Key

A sanctions compliance program will not be effective if it relies only on manual controls. People make mistakes, and manual work requires more staff. That's why automated procedures and applications are essential tools for sanctions compliance. Some processes that may require automation to be an effective control include:

- Scanning System - This is the number one technology a sanctions compliance program needs.
- Environmental Scanning - While a spreadsheet can be used to document the environmental scan process for smaller companies, a risk management system, such as Archer (https://www.archerirm.com/), which we used, is more suitable for larger companies.
- Risk Assessment - While a spreadsheet can be used to document the risk assessment process for smaller companies, a risk management system, such as Archer, which we used, is more suitable for larger companies.
- Training Platform - An automated training platform (i.e., a learning management system) can maintain your sanctions training course, update it easily, automatically roll it out to large groups, and track who has completed it and when. Smaller companies may be able to do this manually, if needed.
- Document Management System - Nowadays, most documents and emails are kept digitally rather than on paper. A document management system is beneficial because it can automatically store documents securely, making them easily accessible to anyone in the company. These systems also automatically back up documents to

ensure their safety. Sanctions-related documents must be retained for a minimum of ten years.

Case Study: Controls for WeExport

Table 4 contains examples of controls identified for WeExport for the sanctions risks.

Table 4. Controls for WeExport

Sanctions Risk	Controls
The company does not identify sanctions issues.	Documented sanctions program approved by the chief compliance officer. The company has a team dedicated to sanctions compliance.
Sanctioned customers are not identified.	Customers are screened at onboarding and periodically thereafter using an automated system. Customer due diligence is conducted at account opening.
Transactions that violate sanctions are conducted.	OFAC watchlist screening of all payment transactions using an automated system.
Employees don't understand sanctions or follow sanctions procedures.	Annual training is required for sanctions compliance staff.
New sanctions requirements are not identified and implemented.	Environmental scanning identifies new sanctions requirements.
Third parties may put the company at risk for sanctions violations	Vendor due diligence is conducted at onboarding Contract provisions prohibit certain activities by vendors, wholesalers, and other third parties doing business on the company's behalf.

11
Assess Controls

Once you've identified all applicable sanctions-related controls, you should assess their effectiveness and sufficiency.

Control Effectiveness

Effectiveness asks if the control functions properly. Does it work consistently, occasionally, or not at all? Or is there no control in place?

A control can be evaluated as "effective," "partially effective," or "ineffective." A partially effective control is in place and somewhat functional, but a gap may still exist. For instance, the claims team may manually scan many, but not all, payments before sending them out. Or, you may scan some, but not all, parties against sanctions watchlists.

An ineffective control isn't performed or doesn't work more often than not. For example, if sanctions training has never been provided to staff.

Residual Risk

You can now assess the residual risk of your sanctions risks, now that the controls have been identified and their effectiveness assessed. As a reminder, residual risk is the likelihood, high, medium, or low, that a sanctions violation will still occur despite the controls being performed. The residual risk will tell you if your controls are sufficient to mitigate the sanctions risk, if additional controls are needed, or if controls need to be revised.

Obviously, the inherent risk will not change if you have no controls to mitigate a risk. A partially effective control may only slightly reduce the risk (moving it from high to medium-high) or may not reduce the risk at all.

You should reassess the residual risk after strengthening these controls or implementing new ones to address the gaps.

Remember, a risk is only reduced if the control is in place, working, and completely mitigates the risk.

Control Sufficiency

After assessing the residual risk, you know whether the control indeed reduced the risk, even if it works effectively. This is considered control sufficiency.

For example, suppose you scan all payments through your automated system, with the data being processed overnight. You verify that the system and scanning are working correctly. This control seems effective in reducing the risk of paying a sanctioned party. However, upon closer examination, you find that wire payments are sent to the bank and processed during the day, before the overnight scan. So, a payment could be issued to an SDN before the match is identified through scanning. Therefore, this control isn't entirely effective because not all transactions are scanned before they are issued. Instead, the control can only be considered partially effective.

Additional Control Measures

You may also want to consider other aspects of your controls, such as whether they are **automated, manual, preventative, or detective**. Here's what these terms mean:

- **Automated controls** are performed without human intervention. For example, the scanning control is automated if you have a sanctions screening application.
- **Manual controls** require a person to perform them. If accounts payable manually scans payee names before sending a wire transfer, that's a manual process.

A control can have both automated and manual elements. For instance, your scanning control might use an automated system, but a person has to manually review any potential matches it generates.

- **Preventive controls** stop a sanctions violation from occurring if performed correctly. For example, if your sanctions screening system automatically stops a payment to a sanctioned party, that's a preventative control.
- **Detective controls** identify a sanctions issue after it has occurred, giving you time to correct it before it becomes a violation. For

example, a manager may review a new account before onboarding to ensure that all necessary due diligence has been completed.

A control can have both preventive and detective elements, although this is less likely.

This analysis helps you assess the strength of your controls. If your entire program relies on manual, detective controls, it's weaker because human error can occur. Manual controls are more prone to mistakes and might not always be performed correctly. Detective controls don't prevent errors from happening in the first place. If a detective control fails, no backup prevents a violation.

A more robust program relies primarily on automated, preventative controls. These don't require human intervention or judgment, and they stop violations from occurring immediately.

Case Study: Control Assessment for WeExport

Table 5 is the assessment for a sample of controls identified for WeExport. A more complete analysis can be found in the completed SRA.

Table 5. Controls assessment for WeExport

<table>
<tr><th>Sanctions risk</th><th>Control</th><th colspan="2">Risk & Controls Analysis</th></tr>
<tr><td rowspan="3">Transactions that violate sanctions are conducted.

Inherent risk: medium-high</td><td rowspan="3">Accounts payable manually screens all wire payments before their release to the bank.</td><td>Manual control</td><td>The accounts payable staff must manually scan the payee's name, as once the payment is sent to the bank, it is automatically released before the nightly automated scan of payments occurs.</td></tr>
<tr><td>Preventative control</td><td>The payee's name is scanned before the wire is released to the bank to be sent.</td></tr>
<tr><td>Risk score</td><td>Partially effective. Staff do not consistently scan wire payments before releasing them to the bank.</td></tr>
<tr><td>Residual risk: medium</td><td></td><td colspan="2">Most payments are automatically scanned by the system, which reduces residual risk. However, not all wire payments are checked before being released to the bank.</td></tr>
</table>

Table 5 (continued).

<table>
<tr><th>Sanctions Risk</th><th>Control</th><th colspan="2">Risk & Controls Analysis</th></tr>
<tr><td rowspan="3">Employees don’t understand sanctions or follow sanctions procedures.

Inherent risk: high</td><td rowspan="3">Annual training is required for sanctions compliance staff.</td><td>Manual control</td><td>Sanctions compliance staff identify and attend training sessions offered by outside organizations.</td></tr>
<tr><td>Preventative controls</td><td>Training helps provide employees with the knowledge they need to comply with sanctions regulations. It does not detect a lack of staff knowledge of sanctions.</td></tr>
<tr><td>Risk score</td><td>Ineffective. Most staff at WeExport who perform sanctions-related controls have received no sanctions training in the last three years.</td></tr>
<tr><td>Residual risk: high</td><td></td><td colspan="2">Control is ineffective, so inherent risk remains unchanged.</td></tr>
<tr><td rowspan="3">Third parties may put the company at risk for sanctions violations.

Inherent risk: medium-high</td><td rowspan="3">Vendor due diligence is conducted at onboarding.</td><td>Manual control</td><td>Information on the potential vendor is obtained and reviewed manually.</td></tr>
<tr><td>Preventative control</td><td>Due diligence is conducted before contracting with a new third party, which helps prevent a risky third party from becoming a contractor.</td></tr>
<tr><td>Risk score</td><td>Partially effective. While due diligence before onboarding is considered adequate, there is no ongoing monitoring of vendors for new sanctions issues during the contract term.</td></tr>
<tr><td>Residual risk: medium</td><td></td><td colspan="2">Residual risk drops slightly to medium due to initial due diligence and scanning of third-party payments.</td></tr>
</table>

As you can see from the analysis in Table 5, there are instances where the controls aren’t working as effectively as expected or don’t exist. The next chapter will explore what to do next.

12
Gap Identification and Remediation

Now that you've identified and assessed the sanctions controls in place, you've arrived at the critical part of the risk assessment: What are your control gaps, why do those gaps exist (i.e., the root cause), and what can you do to close those gaps?

Control Gaps

A control gap happens when the controls don't operate well or are missing altogether. You have a control gap if:

- you have a sanctions risk with no control to mitigate it
- your control isn't functioning effectively
- your control does not adequately cover the risk (sufficiency)
- you have an inherent risk that hasn't been reduced by the control in place

Root Cause Analysis

The first step to remedy this gap is to figure out why it happened. You may hear this referred to as a "root cause analysis," which means identifying the primary or "root" reason why a control deficiency occurred, allowing you to implement an appropriate solution.

Perhaps procedures are outdated, technology is insufficient, resources are inadequate to perform the tasks, or the procedure got dropped when a function was reorganized. All of those can be reasons why a control gap exists.

A common way to conduct this analysis is the Five Whys approach, which means asking "why?" five times to get to the root cause.[31] But you don't need to ask exactly five questions; some issues may be identified more quickly or require more research.

Let's conduct an example root cause analysis using WeExport.

In WeExport's risk assessment, they learned that employees weren't consistently manually scanning payees before sending a wire to the bank. The control is manually screening payees; the gap is that it isn't being performed. When you ask why, you learn it's because employees didn't know they were supposed to. When you again ask why, you learn it's because employees didn't know they were supposed to. When you again ask why, you discover they haven't been trained on the procedure. In fact, no one has trained employees on sanctions for at least three years, and as a result, they don't understand them. This is the root cause of the problem.

Remediation

The last step is to close the gap by redesigning the control or implementing a new one. Document the control gaps in your risk assessment and create a plan to fix them.

Obtain support from senior management for any new procedures. Use your risk assessment to demonstrate to management that these controls are necessary to avoid serious consequences. Sometimes, fixing these issues may require financial investment, which will need approval. This expense might need to be added to next year's budget instead of being fixed immediately.

Collaborate on the new or revised procedures with those responsible for carrying them out. When you create procedures solely based on your vision, they may not be feasible for the staff tasked with implementing them, and they will push back on doing them or not do them at all. Engage with the team from the start; they often have valuable insights on executing the procedures effectively. This approach ensures their initial support for the procedure and increases the likelihood of its success.

Once you've fixed the control gaps, reassess the new and revised controls to ensure they work effectively. Reassess the residual risk to verify that the sanctions risk has decreased due to the new controls. Schedule the reassessment for one to three months in the future to allow time for the controls to take effect and gather data on their effectiveness.

There may be situations where a control gap exists, but remediating the issue would be too costly or burdensome. If the inherent risk of a sanctions risk is not high, the line of business may accept it. This means management is aware of the gap and has decided not to remediate it. The reason for acceptance should be well-documented, in case it ever becomes an issue in court or with OFAC.

Case Study: Control Gaps and Remediation for WeExport

Table 6 assesses a sample of the control gaps identified for WeExport. The remainder can be found in the completed SRA.

Table 6. Control gaps and remediation for WeExport

Control	Control Gap	Remediation Plan
Customer due diligence is conducted at account opening.	There is no review of beneficial ownership.	WeExport will conduct a project to strengthen the customer due diligence process, including developing a method to identify and scan beneficial owners of certain types of customers and reviewing third-party databases of beneficial ownership information to determine if one would be suitable and cost-effective.
Accounts payable manually screens all wire payments before their release to the bank.	Accounts payable staff do not consistently scan wire payments before releasing them to the bank.	Training specific to how and when to complete the manual scan of payees will be created and issued by the end of the year.
Annual training is required for sanctions compliance staff.	Most staff at WeExport have received no sanctions training in the last three years, including staff who perform sanctions-related controls.	A basic sanctions training program will be developed and issued to all company employees.
Environmental scanning identifies new sanctions requirements.	Environmental scan tracking is conducted manually via a spreadsheet. An automated system would be stronger.	None. Management accepts this minor risk. While an automated system would be better for tracking new regulations and their implementation within the company, the cost of a risk management system is currently prohibitive.

13

Risk Assessment Documentation and Next Steps

The final results of your risk assessment should be documented using a spreadsheet or Word document, such as the one provided with this guide. A risk management system, such as Archer (https://www.archerirm.com/), which was used at my prior organization, would likely be more effective for larger companies.

Generally, the company's sanctions compliance officer should share the completed risk assessment with senior management, such as the chief compliance officer, get their approval for any necessary fixes, and keep them informed about the progress of gap remediation. Ongoing discussions should be held between sanctions compliance and senior management regarding changes in the risk profile.

The progress of gap remediation does not need to be included in the risk assessment, but would usually be documented in project plans, progress memos, and related documents.

A risk assessment should be considered a "living document," meaning it should be reviewed and updated regularly or when a significant change occurs. This may occur when new sanctions are imposed, your company's profile changes (such as acquiring a new foreign subsidiary or establishing a new foreign manufacturing facility), or new controls are implemented (for example, when a new automated system is installed). At my prior firm, we revised the risk assessment when we acquired a foreign entity and again when Russia invaded Ukraine.

The SRA should be reviewed and updated at least annually in any case.

Training should also continue on various sanctions topics based on the results of your risk assessment. This ongoing education ensures everyone stays informed and compliant with the latest sanctions regulations and procedures.

Ongoing oversight and controls testing should be conducted to ensure there are no changes to their assessment in your SRA.

Ready to get started assessing your company? Here is the link to download the risk assessment template, along with the final example risk assessment for WeExport: https://easysanctions.wordpress.com/the-plain-english-guide-to-economic-sanctions-risk-assessments/.

14
Conclusion

Developing an economic sanctions risk assessment is crucial in ensuring your organization remains compliant with international regulations and avoids severe penalties. This book has explored the fundamentals of a risk assessment, the importance of a thorough evaluation, and the steps necessary to identify, evaluate, and mitigate sanctions-related risks.

By understanding the specific risks associated with your customers, products, services, and geography, you can create a robust compliance program tailored to your organization's unique needs. Implementing effective controls, continuous monitoring, and regular training will help maintain a high standard of compliance and protect your organization from potential violations.

Remember, a well-executed risk assessment is not a one-time task but an ongoing process that requires vigilance and adaptability. As regulations evolve and your business grows, the risk assessment must adapt to new challenges and opportunities.

I hope this guide has given you the knowledge and tools to develop a comprehensive economic sanctions risk assessment for your organization. By staying proactive and informed, you can navigate the complexities of sanctions compliance with confidence and integrity.

References

Below is a good reference list of websites with additional details on the information provided in this guide.

All OFAC Sanctions Programs
https://ofac.treasury.gov/sanctions-programs-and-country-information

Federal Financial Institutions Examination Council (FFIEC), BSA/AML Manual, Appendix J: Quantity of Risk Matrix
https://bsaaml.ffiec.gov/manual/Appendices/11

FFIEC, BSA/AML Manual, Risk Assessment

https://bsaaml.ffiec.gov/manual/BSAAMLRiskAssessment/01

Free OFAC List Search Tool
https://sanctionssearch.ofac.treas.gov/

OFAC Compliance Guidance for Sanctions Programs
https://ofac.treasury.gov/media/16331/download?inline

OFAC Frequently Asked Questions
https://ofac.treasury.gov/faqs/all-faqs

Artic Intelligence, Sanctions Risk

https://arctic-intelligence.com/risk-domains/sanctions#

Audit Board, Risk Assessment Matrix: Overview and Guide
https://www.auditboard.com/blog/what-is-a-risk-assessment-matrix/

ACAMS Today, Keeping Sanctions-Related Risk Assessments Effective and Current
https://www.acamstoday.org/keeping-sanctions-related-risk-assessments-effective-and-current/

Author Biography

Heidi Hunter worked for a US-based insurance company with global operations for over a decade. She developed and managed the company's sanctions compliance program, covering all its locations. She oversaw the team responsible for complying with sanctions and worked closely with other teams within the company to ensure they understood and followed sanctions regulations. Heidi has a Master of Business Administration (MBA) and is a Certified Public Accountant (inactive).

Visit her website at https://easysanctions.wordpress.com/ for more information on sanctions and to sign up for her newsletter.

All Books in the Plain-English Guide Series by Heidi Hunter

The Plain-English Guide to Economic Sanctions
The Plain-English Guide to Developing an Economic Sanctions Program
The Plain-English Guide to Economic Sanctions Risk Assessments
The Plain-English Guide to Economic Sanctions for Insurance Companies
The Plain-English Guide to Economic Sanctions for Foreign Companies
The Plain-English Guide to Economic Sanctions: The Complete Series

Companion Workbooks:
The Plain-English Guide to Developing an Economic Sanctions Program Workbook
The Plain-English Guide to Economic Sanctions Risk Assessments Workbook

Book and Workbook Bundles:
The Plain-English Guide to Developing an Economic Sanctions Program: Full Guide & Workbook
The Plain-English Guide to Economic Sanctions Risk Assessments: Full Guide & Workbook

Find them all at: https://easysanctions.wordpress.com/books/

If you read one of my guides, please post a rating or review!

Notes

1. OFAC, Frequency Asked Questions, FAQ 12, https://ofac.treasury.gov/faqs/12.

2. OFAC, Frequency Asked Questions, FAQ 12, https://ofac.treasury.gov/faqs/12.

3. Department of the Treasury, "A Framework for OFAC Compliance Commitments," https://ofac.treasury.gov/media/16331/download?inline.

[4]. Due to the end of Bashar al-Assad's regime, on January 6, 2025, OFAC issued General License 24, expanding authorizations for activities and transactions in Syria for an initial six-month period, effective until July 7, 2025. This may lead to the permanent loosening of comprehensive sanctions against Syria.

[5]. OFAC, FAQ 18.

[6]. OFAC, Frequently Asked Questions, FAQ 3, https://ofac.treasury.gov/faqs/all-faqs.

[7]. OFAC, FAQ 3.

[8]. OFAC, FAQ 886.

[9]. OFAC, FAQ 11.

[10]. OFAC, FAQ 10.

[11]. OFAC, FAQ 91.

[12]. Executive Order 13884, "Blocking Property of the Government of Venezuela," August 5, 2019, https://ofac.treasury.gov/media/26786/download?inline.

[13]. OFAC, FAQ 91.

[14]. Department of the Treasury, "Revised Guidance on Entities Owned by Persons Whose Property and Interests in Property Are Blocked," https://ofac.treasury.gov/media/6186/download?inline; OFAC, FAQ 399.

15. Department of the Treasury, "A Framework for OFAC Compliance Commitments."

16 Department of the Treasury, "A Framework for OFAC Compliance Commitments."

17 Department of the Treasury, "A Framework for OFAC Compliance Commitments."

18. Department of the Treasury, "e.l.f. Cosmetics, Inc. Settles Potential Civil Liability for Apparent Violations of the North Korea Sanctions Regulations," January 21, 2019, https://ofac.treasury.gov/media/7041/download?inline.

19. Department of the Treasury, "e.l.f. Cosmetics, Inc. Settles Potential Civil Liability for Apparent Violations of the North Korea Sanctions Regulations," January 21, 2019, https://ofac.treasury.gov/media/7041/download?inline.

20. Auditboard, Risk Assessment Matrix: Overview and Guide," accessed June 18, 2024, https://www.auditboard.com/blog/what-is-a-risk-assessment-matrix/.

21. Vcomply, "What is a Risk Assessment Matrix? How to Create One?" accessed July 11, 2024, https://www.v-comply.com/blog/what-is-risk-assessment-matrix.

22. *BSA/AML Manual*, Appendix J: Quantity of Risk Matrix, Federal Financial Institutions Examination Council (FFIEC), accessed May 8, 2024, https://bsaaml.ffiec.gov/manual/Appendices/11.

23. OFAC, "OFAC Risk Matrix," Economic Sanctions Enforcement Guidelines, 31 C.F.R Part 501, Appendix A, Annex, https://www.ecfr.gov/current/title-31/subtitle-B/chapter-V/part-501/appendix-Appendix_A_to_Part_501.

24. OFAC, Sanctions Programs and Country Information, https://ofac.treasury.gov/sanctions-programs-and-country-information.

25. FATF, "Black and Grey Lists," accessed May 20, 2024, https://www.fatf-gafi.org/en/countries/black-and-grey-lists.html.

26. Transparency International, Corruption Perceptions Index, accessed May 20, 2024, https://www.transparency.org/en/cpi/2023.

27. United States Drug Enforcement Administration, High Intensity Drug Trafficking Areas, https://www.dea.gov/operations/hidta; The White House, "High Intensity Drug Trafficking Areas Program," https://www.whitehouse.gov/wp-content/uploads/2023/06/HIDTA-map-May-2023.pdf.

28. Financial Crimes Enforcement Network, HIFCA Regional Map, https://www.fincen.gov/hifca-regional-map; Comply Advantage, "What Are High Intensity Financial Crime Areas (HIFCAs), https://complyadvantage.com/insights/hifcas/.

29. FinCEN, Beneficial Ownership Information, Frequently Asked Questions, https://www.fincen.gov/boi-faqs.

30. FFIEC, BSA/AML Manual, Office of Foreign Assets Control, Office of Foreign Assets Control—Overview, accessed May 17, 2024, https://bsaaml.ffiec.gov/manual/OfficeOfForeignAssetsControl/01.

31. Wikipedia, "Five Whys" accessed on June 13, 2024, https://en.wikipedia.org/wiki/Five_whys.

www.ingramcontent.com/pod-product-compliance
Lightning Source LLC
LaVergne TN
LVHW022316200926
848481LV00004B/1361